I0786713

Table of Contents

Preamble

California is a nation, with our own distinct culture, history, and homeland. Not a nation in the traditional sense of ethnicity or even linguistics, but as shared believers in an idea called California, a civic project to which every Californian contributes. We are strongest when our diversity of ideas, resources, commerce, and geography are united together as one. People with origins from around the world have come here to live, work, grow, and help build the home we have today.

Meanwhile, we become ever more economically and politically distinct from the federal government of the United States and its distant and indifferent two party electoral system which disenfranchises Californians; they are both unable and disinterested in providing for our unique interests and needs. The California National Party believes the time has arrived for our home to begin its ascent and join the international community while helping to build a stronger and more independent California today.

Why does California need the California National Party now? Primarily, because we believe that the independence of California is a necessity, not only for ourselves, but for the world. For a long time -- and at an accelerated pace in the Internet Age -- California has risen to a central role in both the international economy and the rapidly developing global culture, spurred on by advances in communication and technology. That California is a significant actor in the world is simply a political fact, and such an actor cannot remain a subnational entity for long.

However, until California takes our proper place among the nations, the California National Party believes that our people can only be effectively represented by an organization whose decisions always view the needs and interests of California as its central concern. Forty million people and the world's fifth largest economy deserve and require a political party of their own, away from the influence of two distant corporate-backed parties seeking interests that are not ours. The California National Party is the only party that can say, unequivocally and without reservation, that it seeks to represent the needs and interests of Californians. The Party will always fight for and defend California's people, rights, lives, health, land, resources, and wealth. We seek to benefit the people of California, not the Party's own power. We favor solutions, not ideology.

The need for California to seek ever greater autonomy exists regardless of who holds power in the United States. While it cannot be denied that our open antagonism with the federal government has increased substantially under the present administration, the issues of injustice to California are structural, not situational. Our tax revenue goes to the federal government, which disperses it to states who denigrate us and vote against our interests and values in the national legislature, while we must negotiate for the return of our own money to meet the needs of our people. Our voice in the selection of the president is underrepresented in theory, utterly silenced in practice, since now it is the will of a handful of states that decides the winner. In the Senate—which approves cabinet members, international treaties, and Supreme Court justices—the nearly 40 million people in California have two votes, while the nearly 40 million people in the 22 smallest states have 44 votes. We are the fifth largest economy in the world, but we cannot even make our own trade agreements with other nations. Instead, our commerce and livelihoods depend on decisions made by power holders 2500 miles away, over whom we have little to no control. These problems persist, no matter what party controls Washington DC. The only long-term solution for

California is to secure our income for ourselves and the authority to solve our own problems.

The path to California's necessary and justified independence will likely be a long and arduous one. It will require creative solutions, and the ability for Californians to think beyond the discourse of the party politics of the United States and focus on issues that are important to us, our families, our neighbors, and our future. But it is also one that will further contribute to California's growing sense of identity and unity. Until we succeed at this goal, we in the California National Party look forward to working with the people of our nation and earning the right to represent them, and to propose and enact solutions that improve the lives of all Californians.

Healthcare

The current healthcare system prioritizes profits over patients and is in need of drastic revision. Healthcare is a civil right and should be a promise to all Californians. The California National Party believes that California must move to a universal single-payer system in order to compete with private hospitals, and we will educate Californians about the benefits of single-payer healthcare. The Canadian model, the French model, and the Malaysian model each have strengths and weakness, but all of them are better by far than the American model. The transition to a universal single-payer system will employ the Canadian model at first, and as time goes on California will develop its own system with lessons learned from that experience.

California must end the medical segregation of public health care and consolidate all federal, state, and local healthcare administrations into one unified public system, to be called the California Healthcare System, or CHS. This Medicare-for-all type system will vastly reduce the cost of hospital administration by combining Medicaid, Medicare, the Veterans Administration, workers compensation, Indian Health services and many others into one universal system.

Implementation

Our plan is to institute a functional Medicare-for-all system in 5 to 6 years, and in 15-20 years a new system, most likely similar to what currently operates in France or Malaysia.

The Canadian model will be used in transition, allowing private hospitals to bill the CHS a fee-for-service with rates negotiated by the government, followed by an evolution into a Malaysian or French model once public hospitals are accessible to all. Having a hospital in each county, or in smaller counties a clinic if they choose, and allowing for a managed care system that is all encompassing, will greatly increase access to preventative medicine, and reduce hugely expensive emergency care. To help address the doctor shortage, medical personnel will also be recruited internationally, and medical tourism for Californians will be encouraged.

Pharmaceuticals

The astronomical prices of prescription drugs is a primary driver of rising costs. The CHS should serve as the primary negotiator for medication prices, for all insurers and hospitals, to help control healthcare costs.

California must restrict pharmaceutical advertising, and will enable the CHS to source prescription drugs internationally so as to bring our costs in line with the global average.

Medical Education and Malpractice

California should make healthcare education free for California Residents, forgive existing medical and nursing school debt, and have college students enroll in the CHS Program for Medical Professionals early in their secondary education. This will facilitate the implementation of a more reasonable pay scale.

California must increase the number of doctors by opening additional medical schools and having larger graduating classes.

California needs to implement limited liability insurance for doctors, have the state be partially liable for medical mistakes within the public system, and conduct research as to exactly how many unnecessary deaths and other medical errors are occurring presently. Regular reports on medical malpractice and how to reduce it will maximize the ability of Californians to pursue healthy lifestyles.

Underserved Communities

Healthcare is a civil right that, if not provided to all, is disproportionately denied to those who are less rich, especially people of color. In the interest of focusing on preventative medicine and healthy living, the California National Party believes that California should:

- Return to using house calls for family medicine to limit medical cost, especially in rural areas.

- Direct additional benefits in the form of nutritional assistance and other health necessities to communities of color.

- Establish a statewide system for giving expectant mothers basic material resources and information about childbirth and childrearing.

- Construct community clinics, and incentivize future healthcare investments, in communities of color across the state.

- The California Healthcare System will not reimburse doctors and clinics who refuse patients based on their race, gender, sexuality, disability, religion, or other status unrelated to health.

Immigration

The utterly broken and dysfunctional U.S. immigration system has caused farmers and other businesses to struggle to find workers while the federal government is trying to deport employees, hurting California's economy in the process. It has deported those who have been productive and hard working residents of the state of California. The federal government does not provide an adequate path to citizenship for people who have lived in California for many years, nor do they issue enough temporary guest work visas to keep up with the demands of California's economy. Meanwhile ICE is destroying California families and often causing irreparable harm to the spouses and children of undocumented people when they are ripped from their homes and sent back to countries they often barely know.

The California National Party proposes that the California government create a working group of experts with the goal of enacting a statewide plan to deal with immigration and California residency. This plan should be consistent with the following:

Welcoming Immigrants

California's unique global position allows it to welcome and cultivate diverse peoples and cultures from all over the planet. To that end, the California National Party states that:

- We support the right of California to issue visas to foreign nationals in order to allow them to enter, work, study, and reside in California either with the cooperation of the U.S. Federal Government, or upon independence if the Federal Government refuses to cooperate.
- As soon as is feasible, California shall implement a program to retain in California higher education graduates and other high skilled professionals from other nations as they make us stronger and richer. This program will also include help to find jobs while using the skills and education of such individuals to strengthen California's economy and culture.
- Treat child immigrants as children and not adults. Currently the federal immigration system often perpetuates the fiction that children make choices that they do not actually make, in violation of the UN Charter. Children brought to California do not have the ability to

be considered adults able to make such
decisions, and they should rather be treated
with the compassion and decency that is the
right of all children.

- California must guarantee the right to public
education, including higher education, for all
children in California regardless of
immigration status.

- The California National Party opposes the
construction of any wall along the southern
border of California. If such a wall is built, it
should be removed at the earliest time such
action is feasible.

- Modify Free Trade Agreements to ease the
movement of people across borders, especially
with Mexico, Canada, and Pacific Rim nations.

- California must work with all stakeholders to
improve the economies of its neighbors, in a
mutually beneficial way, in order to reduce the
need for immigration. In order to accomplish
this goal, California shall create an investment
fund to help all neighboring countries, and all
countries with substantial yearly California
immigration, to develop such that their
economies grow, and help California's grow, in
order to reduce the need for immigration into
California.

Residency Permits

- To anyone who has five contiguous years of residency in California, committed no felony in California during that period, and who intends to remain in California indefinitely, California shall issue a residency permit that will allow that individual to legally work and live in California. The residency permit shall also grant the right of any such California resident who is at least 18 years of age to vote in local and state elections in California.

- All agents of the State of California shall be instructed to respect California residency permits so issued, to never turn over any holder of such a permit to any federal immigration agents under any circumstances, and to not interfere with any Californian who holds a duly issued residency permit.

- No language requirement shall be imposed to obtain a California residency permit nor, later, for Californian citizenship. Upon independence, anyone holding a California residency permit will be issued full citizenship in the California Republic.

Guest Worker Program

- California should create a guest worker program operated by the counties in order to best meet their needs. These programs will be coordinated by a state-wide agency.
- Each county shall submit a guest worker program proposal that outlines its guest worker labor needs. Counties can also choose to not seek any guest workers if they have no such needs.
- California shall implement this plan as soon as is feasible, either with the cooperation of the U.S. Federal Government, or upon independence, if the Federal Government refuses to cooperate in this county-based guest worker program.

Environment

California's natural beauty and abundant resources must be preserved for future generations, while being managed in a way that enables stable growth and a prosperous society.

The California National Party recognizes that climate change is the greatest challenge to have ever faced humanity. Minimizing its impacts and mitigating those effects we cannot avoid will require substantial changes to the way we live, work, and do business. California is uniquely positioned to be a global leader in this space and our public policies will reflect this. These adjustments to our lifestyle will not always be easy, but they are needed to avoid an ecological apocalypse in our lifetimes.

As a general statement of our commitment to sustainability, we believe that all activities with potential public health consequences should be guided by the principle of the least toxic alternative, which presumes that toxic substances will not be used as long as there is another way of accomplishing the task.

Climate

Reducing the carbon footprint of every household, factory, and farm is the most important and most difficult task before us. To minimize climate-related natural disasters such as floods, hurricanes, and wildfires, we must rethink the way we live, work, and travel. With this as our organizing principle we advocate for the following policies:

- California Carbon Market: The cap-and-trade system instituted by the California Air Resources Board (CARB) in 2013 should continue to expand, and the governor should actively seek to enroll additional domestic and international partners. The true cost to the environment of consuming fossil fuels has been externalized for far too long, and there is widespread agreement that cap-and-trade is the simplest usable mechanism for pricing these emissions.
- Sea level rise: By the year 2100, the midrange prediction for sea level rise is 36 inches. If these predictions hold the San Francisco Ferry Building will flood twice daily at high tide, and large sections of the Bay Area could flood dozens of times each year. To address this risk,

a new seawall will be constructed at or near the Golden Gate Bridge.

- C40: California cities will be encouraged to join the C40 Cities Climate Leadership Group, an international network of cities that seeks to 'collaborate effectively, share knowledge and drive meaningful, measurable and sustainable action on climate change.'

- Transportation: Transportation is a significant contributor to greenhouse gas emissions. See our Infrastructure Plank for our ideas on evolving California's systems.

Water

With more than 800 miles of Pacific Coast, California has a unique role to play in the protection of marine resources. As this is a shared resource susceptible to exploitation, we should seek to reinforce the long-lasting peaceful alliances with our Pacific neighbors, to ensure continued viability of the ocean as a rich source of food, as well as its inherent integrity as a biome. In particular the following policies are suggested:

- Offshore drilling: We support a permanent moratorium on the extraction of fossil fuels from the seabed, both to avoid short-term damage to the environment and as part of our move towards a post-hydrocarbon energy system.

- Great Garbage Patch: There is a gigantic swirling morass of plastic trash in the North Pacific. To address this, California should mandate the development and use of biodegradable plastics. As well, consumer products that make a significant contribution to this problem, such as microplastics in facial scrubs, should be regulated in a manner that recognizes and seeks to minimize their long-term damage to the environment.

- Marine mammals: Whales, dolphins, seals and porpoises provide essential ecosystem services in terms of nutrient cycling and maintenance of the species balance. Sadly, many of these populations are at risk due to degradation of their habitat and overfishing of their prey. To ensure their indefinite survival, practices that endanger these animals, such as indiscriminate commercial fishing and the use of low-frequency sonar, will be heavily regulated. On land and at sea, to provide an adequate food source for orcas, viable wild salmon populations will be favored, within reason, at the expense of economic interests.

- Public Beach Access: In accordance with California precedent established by the Spanish and dating back to Roman times, the portion of the land covered by the sea at high tide will be held in trust by the state for the benefit, use, and enjoyment of the public.

California's river systems must also be well managed to ensure sustainable use for irrigators, wildlife, and other consumers of water. Towards this end we encourage the removal of obsolete dams, close monitoring of water quality, and an ongoing dialogue with industrial, residential, and agricultural consumers so that riparian systems can continue to function with biological integrity while continuing to meet the needs of California's human population.

Agriculture

California is a unique contributor to agriculture in North America and around the world due to the high quality and wide variety of crops grown here, in particular fruits and nuts. Many of these crops, especially wine grapes, are highly sensitive to small changes in environment and could be devastated by climate change. Modern farming is an energy and labor intensive exercise, and California should continue to lead the way in developing sensible regulations to protect farms, farmworkers, and the environment. Specifically:

- Integration with the Carbon Market: The impact of land management techniques such as no-till, low-till, crop rotation and the use of cover crops will be evaluated in terms of greenhouse gas emission or absorption, so that practices that incorporate atmospheric CO_2 back into the soil will be rewarded, and taxes levied against practices that do not.
- Nutrient bookkeeping: The legislature will draft regulations requiring farms to demonstrate they are not polluting surface waters through application of excess fertilizer.
- Genetically Modified Organism (GMO) labeling: While transgenic foods are recognized as safe by the vast majority of scientists, many people strongly object to their consumption. Therefore we propose a system of voluntary labelling where producers may include a GMO-free marking on their products, with compliance to be overseen by a third party such as the Non-GMO Project.
- Breeder's Rights and Farmer's Privilege: In recognition that our food supply is increasingly controlled by a small group of

large corporations, CNP supports the rights of small seed companies and individual farmers to develop plant varieties that are well-suited to their local conditions and market demands. California should continue to regulate this field in a manner consistent with the International Convention for the Protection of New Varieties of Plants. In particular, the legislature should exercise the optional clause found in Article 15.2, which protects the ability of breeders to profit from their development of new varieties, and also enables a signatory to "restrict the breeder's right in relation to any variety in order to permit farmers to use for propagating purposes, on their own holdings, the product of the harvest which they have obtained by planting, on their own holdings."

Conservation

California is a biologically diverse place with many rare and endemic species, due to our wide variety of micro-climates, topography, and natural barriers to migration. The California National Party believes that preserving our biodiversity is important not only from an ethical and aesthetic perspective but also for ecological, economic and medicinal reasons. We believe that it is possible to harmonize human activity with conservation, resulting in thriving human communities within thriving natural ecosystems, and so we call on California's lawmakers to do the following:

- Incorporate into environmental policy the economic value of ecosystem services such as pollination, flood control, carbon sequestration and the natural control of pest species.
- Begin proceedings to turn over all federal lands in California to the government of California. The federal government has failed in their duty to protect and preserve our wild spaces, and our domestic park service could do a far better job without their interference.
- Preserve and expand public lands in response to climate change, while allowing for sustainable development.
- Continue to responsibly regulate the harvest of wildlife both on land and at sea.
- Provide financial incentives for the preservation of habitat on private lands, as Brazil has done to protect primary forests.
- Support ongoing research to detect and eradicate invasive species before they become a threat to native ecosystems.

- Place an immediate and permanent ban on fracking within California. Fracking encourages dependency on fossil fuel technology, endangers our water supply, and causes earthquakes.

Healthy forests are essential for healthy streams and water systems, which in turn support our fisheries. They also provide critical carbon sequestration and habitat for endangered species, and California's wild places draw millions of tourists every year. To protect and preserve them for the indefinite future, we advocate that:

- California end clear-cutting, strip mining, and the privatization of public lands so that public resources are available for the public.
- We should mimic Germany's approach to forest management which relies on selective logging to reduce fire risk, instead of cutting down entire sections of forest and replanting with monoculture.

Education

Schools, colleges, and universities in California should be run by administrators who are also educators with teaching experience, not politicians or non-academic managers. There shall be a moratorium placed on increased administrative spending, and in particular an end to increasing senior administrator pay, until tuition costs and pay issues for educators are resolved. Ongoing training, including leadership skills and professional development, must be accessible so all teachers can stay up to date on new knowledge and provide the best quality instruction, while also creating a path for teachers to move into administration.

All levels of public education in California must have a California studies component, covering such topics as California history, government, culture, geography, art, etc. College and university students would be required to pass a class in California politics to receive their degrees, just as is presently required for American Government.

Pre-K through High School

The California National Party supports universal Pre-Kindergarten education. This includes expanding the current public school system to include non-compulsory full-day Kindergarten and free full-day preschool for 3 and 4-year olds.

Beyond Pre-Kindergarten and Kindergarten, we will develop California-wide standards for history and science curricula using material crafted independently of the American market, specifically the "Texas curriculum" which is the basis of most U.S. textbooks. Such education must focus on the variety of contributions to world, North American, and California history, made by people of many ethnic, political, and gender backgrounds.

- The accomplishments of our ancestors would be celebrated and historic injustices acknowledged.
- Science curriculum would be based on facts currently and widely accepted by the global scientific community in such fields as biology, astronomy, environmental geography, etc.
- Emphasis would be on the development of critical thinking skills and the practice of evaluating evidence.
- Investment in STEM fields, with emphasis on historically underrepresented groups.

- Educate all students in English and Spanish, the two primary languages of the Western Hemisphere, with a goal of bilingual fluency.
- Additional resources devoted to study of languages of increasing global importance, e.g. Mandarin Chinese, Hindustani, etc. taught through a combination of in class study and an online curriculum so students are not limited by local resources.
- Fine arts, music, technology, and cyber-safety courses will also be required, from Kindergarten through High School.

While we realize that the primary function of public education is to prepare young people to enter the workforce, we feel it is also important to instill an appreciation for music and fine arts. These programs are typically the first to be cut in a budget crisis, and are difficult to restart once finances improve. Therefore we suggest that all California primary schools be required to maintain some level of programming in these areas, and that they be valued equally with athletic programs when funding priorities are set.

The California National Party also advocates:

- Overhauling teacher retention and review policies, to support new teachers and keep them working within the K-12 system.
- Teachers must be guaranteed academic freedom and have their performance evaluated using a review standard that includes peers, superiors, and students to ensure quality instruction.
- Providing teachers the ability to move to different districts while maintaining seniority and pay grade.
- Ensuring consistent standards of quality between districts, with a maximum funding difference of 15% per student between school districts, allowing flexibility to provide higher salaries in more expensive areas while guaranteeing that no schools are left underfunded.

College and University

All Community Colleges should be free for Californians, regardless of immigration status, as defined in the Immigration plank. The Community College system would be intended as not only the first stage of higher education for young adults to decide their educational path, gain employable vocational skills, etc., but also for adult retraining programs as the economy continues to evolve, as well as general educational enrichment for all Californians.

The California National Party will:

- Create in California, similar to the German or Canadian models, a supervised and regulated apprentice program combining academic course work with paid, on-site job training for both blue-collar and white-collar employment, leading to an Associate's Degree and job placement.
- Guarantee admission to the California State University (CSU) anywhere in California all students who do not already possess a Bachelor's degree and fulfill certain class requirements within a given time period with at least a 2.5 GPA in academic classes.
- Guarantee admission to the University of California (UC) those with a 3.3 GPA, if they prefer.
- Guarantee transfer agreements with at least one CSU and one UC from each Community College.

- Ensure that tuition for transfer students will be covered in subsequent academic periods so long as the above GPAs are maintained.
- Ensure that other students are permitted to apply, and tuition costs should be reduced from their current level and capped.
- See to it that student fees and acceptance policy for non-Californians would remain unchanged.

Students graduating from a California high school with a 3.3 GPA for CSUs and 3.5 for UCs can enter university directly if they wish and will have tuition waived if they maintain those GPAs for their freshman/sophomore years, and will then be subject to the GPA requirements for transfer students. Since this will vastly reduce the number of incoming students, the size of freshman/sophomore classes at CSUs and UCs will be smaller.

California will undertake an expansion of the Community College system, especially in rural areas, and see to it that, just as each county should have a county hospital, each county with a population over 50,000 should have its own community college system. Smaller counties will be unified into districts with physical classes held at locations in each county.

Smaller expansions of the CSU and UC system should also cover greater geographic diversity and we propose the following campuses: CSU Redding, Indio, Hanford (near the location of the proposed Kings-Tulare Regional Station), and UC Visalia.

Finally, post-graduation, we must reduce tuition for graduate degrees at CSUs and UCs, with an optional program to waive or reduce tuition in exchange for a period of employment in county hospitals, district attorney and public defender offices, the California public education system, etc. depending on degree.

The California National Party believes that California should:

- Incorporate critical ethnic and racial studies into all K-16 education.
- Maintain education as a fundamental civil right and an essential process for understanding the world, which is unfortunately currently devoid of thinking critically, and of learning about racism.
- Establish comprehensive statewide ethnic/racial issue education standards for primary, secondary, and tertiary public and private schools.

- Mandate that accurate history classes and at least one additional language (beyond the student's native language) be taught to all students, beginning in primary education.
- Increase funding for elective foreign language instruction at all levels of public education.
- Incentivize study abroad programs in secondary schools that are fully-accessible to all students, regardless of socioeconomic status.
- Guarantee high performing teachers the ability to move from one district to another.
- Increase funding of new teacher salaries with a focus on underserved areas, and with an explicit ban on using increased funding for administrator and veteran teacher salaries, or for facilities costs.

Civil Rights

California must reassert respect for the civil rights of all its citizens. In a Republic governed by a Constitution, all legal codes must be coherent with that primary document, and its citizens and institutions -- including governmental, military, and corporate entities -- must have equal access to justice and be treated equally under the law.

As a nation, California must do better to ensure that our young people have the opportunity to reach their full potential. We cannot guarantee equality of outcomes, but everyone should have equal opportunities and not have their destiny determined by their zip code at birth. This commitment to justice will be reflected in all our policy positions and actions.

Rights of Women

The ability of women to become leaders in their communities is fundamental not only to the empowerment of women, but the creation of a fair and just society for all citizens. Supporting and promoting women in all their roles in a community, from their employment to their private lives and choices, is crucial for creating a culture in which all citizens are treated fairly, succeed in their lives, and contribute to the sense that everyone matters.

In the last few years we have seen how the increased participation by women in the political sphere, as well as breaking barriers in taking up jobs traditionally reserved for men, has been a force of political and social change in California. The California National Party is committed to advocating for policies which will continue to promote the rights of women, to encourage women to participate in the political process, and to continue to educate the public about the barriers faced by women and the role of political policies in defining and supporting the rights of women.

Workplace Policies

Workplace issues include equal pay, equal opportunity in hiring and promotion, appropriate policies for adjudication of sexual and racial discrimination, harassment and retaliation, and fair access to training programs. While California leads the nation in legislation regarding equal pay, California women continue to lose an estimated $78.6 billion every year due to the wage gap.

To address this inequality, we will do the following:

- Support equal and proportional access for
  women of all ages to training, jobs and
  promotions, capital, equity, and support in the
  creation of businesses.
- Support affirmative action, the rights accorded
  to women in Title IX, 20 USC section 1681 et
  seq, the UN contract resulting from the
  Convention on the Elimination of All Forms of
  Discrimination Against Women (CEDAW)
  commencing in 1979, and ratification of the
  Equal Rights Amendment (ERA) to the U.S.
  Constitution.
- Require that all businesses formed or
  operating in the State of California with 50
  employees or more provide bi-annual reports
  to the State certifying the general equity and
  pay equality conditions in their workplace.
- Require that all corporations receiving any
  government contract from any state or
  municipal agency have at least 40 percent of its
  board members be women.
- Encourage women and provide resources to
  women, particularly women from ethnic
  minority, LGBTQ, and disabled communities,
  to run for public office, and promote and
  emphasize the need for equal representation in
  public office from local levels to the highest

state and federal levels, including in police forces and the judiciary.

- Require that all educational materials used in classrooms in public and private schools include women's history and promote gender equity.

Birth Control and Access to Safe, Legal Abortions

The CNP supports the long established policy that it is a woman's right to control her reproductive choices. Birth control must be covered by all insurances, regardless of whether it is funded by and procured through a woman's employer, including employers who object to birth control or abortion, or through individually obtained plans. The CNP will continue to keep abortions safe and legal in California and opposes any future threats to these protections.

Specifically, the California National Party will:

- Preserve confidential, unrestricted access to affordable, high quality, culturally sensitive health care services, including the full range of reproductive services, contraception and abortion, without requiring guardian, parental, or male partner's consent or notification, or government intervention in any reproductive decision.

- Require that all businesses in California, including health care providers and insurance companies, charge women and men equal rates.
- Require sex education in school curriculum in California, including education on sexually transmitted diseases, for all schools receiving public funds.
- Require pharmaceutical companies to test the efficacy and safety of all drugs using women subjects in research studies, not just men.

Violence Against Women

From 2015 to 2017, the California Partnership to End Domestic Violence reported that approximately 40% of California women experienced domestic violence at some point in their lives. According to the California Coalition Against Sexual Assault, there were an estimated 2 million female victims of rape living in California, and an estimated 8.6 million survivors of sexual violence other than rape in California.

Human trafficking is a form of modern slavery that occurs in every state, including California. Sex trafficking constitutes over 75% of the trafficking cases in CA, with women being the victim almost 90% of the time. While the California Penal Code prohibits individuals from profiting from the business of sex workers, "pimping" continues to exist.

California has an obligation to eliminate violence against its women citizens. Tougher laws regarding violence towards women are needed, as well as programs initiated to prevent violence against women. Gender inequality allows for this violence to continue unabated, unpunished, and sometimes entirely unnoticed. Women should not have to wait years before having their abusers prosecuted, or before receiving assistance to leave an abusive situation.

In 2017, California strengthened its laws on sexual assault, including eliminating the statute of limitations for sexual assault, assigning mandatory prison time for offenders whose victims were unconscious at the time of the assault, and changing from misdemeanors to felonies the possession of certain drugs, like ketamine. The California National Party supports such efforts and is dedicated to adding tougher laws regarding sexual assault and violence against women.

Specifically, the California National Party does:

- Recognize that freedom and protection from violence or abuse, domestic and otherwise, is a fundamental right.
- Support the programs of the U.S. Violence Against Women Act (VAWA), 42 USC Section 13701 et seq., including educational and preventive initiatives, especially those that serve women at risk of sexual and domestic violence.
- Encourage the recognition that gun violence in domestic violence is a public health issue requiring mental and physical health treatment and intervention.
- Facilitate the awareness that the harassment of women in public by deed or verbally (such as catcalling) has a negative impact on the women involved and on a culture that tolerates such behavior.
- Support legislation such as AB 2034 which requires businesses exposed to trafficking to provide their employees with training on how to recognize the signs of human trafficking and how to report those signs to the appropriate law enforcement agency.

- Enforce current laws proscribing the exploitation of sex workers while decriminalizing sex work itself so workers can report abuses without fear of legal penalty; and begin exploring the legalization, regulation, and taxation of the voluntary sex worker industry.
- Work to increase availability of comprehensive educational and training programs for formerly incarcerated women to enhance parenting and job skills.

Maternity/Paternity Leave

At the present time, under the U.S. Family and Medical Leave Act (FMLA), companies with more than 50 employees are required to provide unpaid, job-protected leave for family and medical reasons with continuation of group health insurance under the same terms and conditions as if the employee had not taken leave. This includes 12 workweeks of leave for the birth and care of a child in its first year.

Employers with at least five employees must give employees a reasonable period of leave (generally six to eight weeks) for disability relating to pregnancy, childbirth, or related conditions. This period is not to exceed four months. Also, California extends FMLA to same-sex couples, and the state's disability program allows eligible workers to claim up to 55% of their wages while out on medical leave.

The California National Party supports these policies, and will actively oppose any proposed weakening of them in the future.

Additionally, we advocate for:

- Paid paternity leave for fathers for the same amount of time as that of maternity leave, and the same percentage of wages, no matter what the size of the company. Currently, paternity leave is only offered by about 24 percent of companies, and only averages about 22 days in length, while only about 36 percent of men take advantage of it.

- Employers must provide their full-time, year-round workers at least three weeks of paid vacation each year.

- Employers must also provide full-time workers at least one week of paid sick leave each year, so that women and men can stay home when they are ill, or to care for sick children.

- The expansion of workplace rights for women, including flextime, compensatory time, and pregnancy and family leave.

Child Care Available to All Californians

The California National Party is committed to ensuring that quality cost-free or low-cost child care is available to all Californians, regardless of employment, insurance, citizenship status, or any other factors. The cost of quality child care is currently out of reach for many Californians.

Specifically, we will:

- Establish CA Childcare and Education Savings Accounts (CESA) into which California deposits funds for each child in the household to be used by their caregivers exclusively for child care, regardless of income.

- Promote proper training, certification, equipment, facilities, and employment of child care professionals in all areas where they are needed.

Addressing Structural Racism

As an organization, the California National Party will place particular emphasis on including and empowering communities that historically have been marginalized. While great strides have been made in reducing racism and other forms of bias, work remains to be done. Much of this social change lies outside the realm of politics and cannot and should not be addressed through laws that attempt to dictate how people act towards one another. However, where structural bias exists it is the duty of the state to identify and remedy it, so as to develop a system that does not unfairly discriminate and guarantees equal access to justice.

Towards that end, California must guarantee equality of opportunity for all, regardless of race, religion, sexual orientation, gender identity, gender, class, disability, or other status. At the legislative level, this should include equal pay for equal work, legal protections against discrimination, and robust mechanisms for addressing harassment and other symptoms of cultural bias. Women and gender-nonconforming people of color in particular experience the intersections of both sexism and racism, which mandates additional support to empower and liberate them.

Economic Justice

A lack of jobs, unequal pay, unequal education, hiring discrimination, historical disinvestment, and capital flight from communities of color has severely damaged the capability of people of color to find and keep jobs that pay a living wage. The California National Party believes that California should take expansive affirmative action to assist communities of color, with an emphasis on black communities, via the following actions:

- Provide free vocational training to adults or the formerly incarcerated through strategic expansion of existing CalWORKS programs.
- Implement robust tax breaks and credits specific to minority-owned small businesses.
- Implement a micro-credit loan system for individuals with education or experience in business and who produce viable risk-assessed business plans.
- Create a hedge and/or sovereign wealth fund specifically for reinvestment in communities of color, via the publicly-owned Bank of the Republic of California.

Diversified Representation

Collecting and categorizing information is a core function of any government, and yet most data is either poorly analyzed or not collected in the first place. This lack of clarity on racial issues is compounded by a broader lack of people of color working in city, county, and state government. The California National Party believes that California should:

- Collect disaggregated demographic data on all its residents and recognize additional ethnic categories beyond the simplistic ones currently in use.
- Expand data collection on police use of force and policing more generally.
- Implement affirmative action hiring initiatives for executive- and mid-level positions across all state and county agencies.

Rights of First Nation Californians

The California National Party respects the sovereign rights of First Nation Californians and must exert pressure on the federal government to do the same. To begin making reparations for the genocide that has been perpetrated against First Nation Californians,

we support the doubling in size of all First Nations'
lands in order to provide some compensation for past
crimes. Where possible, all land returned will come
from the 45% of California currently controlled by the
federal government. If any present owners must be
displaced, which will be avoided if it is practical, they
will be paid fair market value for their land.

As California becomes independent, First Nation
Californians should have the option to either re-assert
their right to autonomy and self-rule, or to
voluntarily join the Republic of California, as
determined by a vote of each group's members.

Rights of the Disabled

Disability is a normal part of life. The California
National Party supports the inclusion of people with
disabilities in society and the elimination of barriers
to that inclusion.

Right to Healthcare

In terms of the health and medical needs of people
with disabilities, the California National Party is
committed to comprehensive universal healthcare, as
a civil right. When enacted as law and policy,
universal health care will ameliorate many of the

hardships, stresses and fears faced by people with disabilities. It will also cast aside the current perverse system where a person with a disability has to remain impoverished to qualify for Medi-Cal or other health care programs.

Right to Community Inclusion

We stand opposed to the institutionalization of people with disabilities and seniors and believe that keeping people in their homes and their communities is a priority for a civil society. Programs that support communal inclusion, like In Home Supportive Services, must be funded at adequate levels to assure that people with disabilities can reach their potential and safely remain in their homes if they choose to do so.

Policies within social safety net programs that treat beneficiaries as "suspects" must be eliminated. Though preventing fraud and abuse is important part of any program, being impacted by a disability is not a crime. Providing every adult with a basic income will do more than anything else to stabilize these at-risk populations. We also support generous tax credits for families caring for aging relatives or family members with chronic illnesses or disabilities.

Californians with Disabilities Act

We support the expansion of the civil rights of people with disabilities through enacting a Californians with Disabilities Act (CDA). The CDA will build upon existing California statutes to provide protection that exceeds the federal Americans with Disabilities Act (ADA) of 1990 and protects the rights of people with disabilities in the workplace, public accommodations, and governmental programs, services and activities. Other California laws that protect the rights of people with disabilities, such as the Fair Employment and Housing Act, will be harmonized with the CDA, or left in place and bolstered.

California should be able to assure justice for people with disabilities without having to rely on a patchwork of state and federal law. The CDA will be tailored for our society. Education about the rights of people with disabilities and enforcement of the CDA will include a public sector enforcement component so that civil litigation is not the only method to achieve access and justice. We also support robust tax credits for small businesses seeking to become accessible to people with disabilities and comply with the law.

There is a strong correlation between mental illness and poverty and homelessness. This is particularly true in minority communities. California cities must end the practice of providing homeless with one-way bus tickets, as this merely relocates individuals at risk. We are committed to ending the use of police and jails as the principle modality for addressing mental illness. In particular, ending the private prison experiment will reduce the financial incentive to incarcerate people with drug addictions, many of whom are undiagnosed and unmedicated.

We support California's entry into the Convention on the Rights of Persons with Disabilities (CRPD), an international norm that was rejected by the United States Senate. Until the day we can enter the CRPD as a sovereign nation, California will voluntarily abide by the CRPD and advocate for the United States to enter that convention.

Prosperity and Growth

California is a major world power. Our economic
policies need to reflect the size and scope of our
economy, and our values, both at home and abroad.
We are the 5th largest economy in the world, yet still
have a higher poverty rate than any other state.
Clearly, our system can evolve in a way that ensures
our continued global prominence, and creates a better
standard of living for all Californians.

California must get a fair deal until we separate from
the United States. Currently, we receive far less from
DC than we send to it each year. We demand an
immediate end to this unjustifiable policy. California
can no longer be expected to subsidize other states
and reckless federal spending while our own needs
go unmet.

California, with a dynamic economy that includes
both Silicon Valley and the Central Valley, is afflicted
with a persistently high level of income inequality.
We should examine ways to reduce this inequality,
and to limit the immense power that is wielded by
individuals whose wealth derives from stock options
and initial public offerings. In order to stimulate
economic growth, we advocate progressive taxation

and a simplification of the tax code. All types of income should be taxed, and in a way that encourages people to invest wealth instead of hoarding it. The current system has led to an unsustainable situation in which the public looks to billionaires to solve problems, rather than seeking to create community-based solutions to issues that affect everyone.

We advocate universal health care as outlined in our healthcare platform. This removes the burden from businesses of paying for employee healthcare, which in turn removes a major barrier to entry for startups and small businesses.

Universal Basic Income

California should adopt a Universal Basic Income, or UBI, for all citizens. Automation, the growth of robotics, and artificial intelligence means that fewer human workers will be needed in the future. Left to its own devices, the free market has no reason to provide a livelihood to persons who are not necessary for its function, and so the government must provide social benefits in order to avoid a humanitarian crisis. Persistent poverty, homelessness, and crime are just some of the blights upon society that can occur when people are replaced by technology and have nowhere else to turn.

Our current federal and state social welfare and unemployment insurance programs are costing us nearly $100 billion per year according to the Congressional Budget Office. The administration of CalFresh, Section 8, welfare, WIC, Medicaid, and many other anti-poverty programs requires a tremendous bureaucracy, and absorbs a large percentage of the tax dollars that should be delivered to those in need. Despite this, poverty is still rampant and frequently an increase in earnings results in a decrease in benefits, sending families into a "poverty trap".

To address this the California National Party endorses the study and subsequent implementation of UBI. With UBI every adult citizen receives a modest monthly payment regardless of earnings or any other "means testing". When designed correctly, this will dramatically reduce welfare administrative costs as the myriad of programs are replaced by simply issuing standardized cash payments. It would also eliminate the time and stress suffered by welfare recipients as they attempt to navigate the complexities of the current system, which should enable more efficient pursuit of economic activity. It is not the intent of UBI to provide a luxurious standard of living, rather to ensure that no one goes without housing, food, and other basic needs due to circumstances beyond their control or even their own poor life choices.

In addition to better managing tax dollars, UBI spurs art and innovation and empowers individuals to seek a job that suits them, rather than desperately clinging to one out of fear of homelessness and starvation. Importantly, with full UBI there is no need for a minimum wage, which imposes a tremendous burden on small businesses and distorts the labor market.

This is a very ambitious goal and will require a great deal of careful experimentation. It will be expensive, however the monies distributed via UBI will almost immediately be spent and re-spent locally, not stashed away in an offshore account. The city of Stockton, with a grant from Facebook, has recently begun the first trial of UBI in California. We will be watching the results closely and hope to draw on their experience in developing a plan for state-wide implementation.

Public Bank

California should create a state-owned bank that will hold our gold and other precious metal reserves, manage the Innovation and Equity Funds described below, provide banking services to all Californians, and allow industries which are legal in California yet still illegal or over-regulated in the rest of the United States to have access to banking services. The bank, which we suggest calling the Bank of the Republic of California, will be subject to independent audits every 5 years.

We propose a ban on high-interest payday loan and check cashing businesses that prey on poor and working class people, and charge unconscionable fees for basic services. We propose to instead add branches of the public bank in each county to ensure that all Californians have access to low-cost banking services in their local communities.

California Innovation Fund

We advocate for the creation of an Office of Innovation whose mandate is to find ways to leverage technology to make government more responsive, efficient, and democratic. This office will administer an Innovation Fund that provides funding for science and pure research, in-line with what the most progressive EU nations provide. California should retain patents on technology created, license those patents to businesses that pay taxes in California at a discount in order to encourage tech companies to locate here, and apply the profits towards an endowment for the fund to help it grow and become self-sustaining over time. This innovation fund can also finance research aimed at improving desalination and clean energy technologies that are critical for California's long-term security.

We encourage cities and counties to create publicly-owned broadband services. These efforts should be woven together in order to create a California-wide system of public broadband that should seek to be the fastest and most affordable broadband in the world.

We advocate for the legislature to facilitate the deployment of autonomous vehicles through sensible regulations regarding their use and funding for additional research and development.

Address Economic Inequality

California should encourage entrepreneurship among working class communities where people lack the skills and social networks that make so many startups possible for those who are already wealthy. California should fund free public classes on how to start and run a business successfully; and offer counseling on obtaining financing, including from the public bank.

California will make micro-credit loans available through the public bank to individuals who complete courses or have equivalent experience and can produce a viable risk-assessed business plan, as well as meeting other reasonable requirements. Micro-credit loans have been proven effective at bringing people, women in particular, out of poverty all over the world. They also have very high payback rates.

We support the creation of a fund, held by the public bank whose mandate is to provide financing, counseling, and logistical support to workers who want to buy their workplaces and turn them into democratically run cooperatives. These would be owned by the employees, not the government, and the loans would be paid back with interest to cover administration costs. Worker-owned businesses do not export jobs and are less likely to downsize workers. They pay living wages, contribute significantly more to community organizations, and have happier, healthier workforces. California has thousands of worker-owned businesses and would benefit from thousands more.

Changing technology means whole industries are becoming obsolete and the average worker will change industries multiple times. We need our workforce to be able to re-train to effectively seize new opportunities. Therefore we advocate government support for mid-career retraining. This must include investment into adult education and community college courses, particularly STEM, to help people change careers and move into fast-growing sectors of the economy. Public-private partnerships will be created to help place graduates of these programs into the workforce.

We will implement measures to ensure access to these programs for low-income and working class people. This includes scholarships, cost of living supports, transportation costs, and low-interest loans, as well as counseling and placement resources. Every struggling family should be provided with the tools needed to overcome poverty.

The California government must support and defend the right of workers to organize for collective bargaining, forming unions, and advocating for their collective interests.

Marijuana Industry

Marijuana must remain legal for use by responsible adults in their own homes throughout California, and this right must be recognized by every county.The National Bank of the Republic of California will engage in transactions with the marijuana industry as it would with any other legal and legitimate business.

However, counties and cities will retain the right to restrict or ban sales, disallow public consumption, limit or even refuse permits for commercial operations, and set local tax rates, in addition to the California tax, to fund local programs.

Like all sectors of the agriculture industry, marijuana growers, processors, and distributors must follow employment, environmental, and business law at both the California and county level. Counties can call on assistance from the California government to enforce compliance of county laws regarding such violations.

Gas Tax

Automobiles are different in many ways in rural and urban regions, most especially in more sparsely populated, decentralized counties where mass transit options are limited if not absent. Many of these areas also have a lower median income level compared to more urbanized regions. As such, the current system of a flat, California-wide gas tax is a clear form of regressive taxation that disproportionately impacts these communities.

The California National Party will seek to set a hard limit on the California excise tax on gasoline as a percentage of not more than 8%, immediately reducing gas costs. These funds are to be used only for transportation infrastructure, primarily for projects that span over multiple counties or are necessary transit or commercial corridors. The California government will then disperse additional funds to counties for construction and development based on factors such as population, demonstrable need, frequency and volume of both local and transient use, etc.

Counties would then also be permitted set their own local gas sales tax to be used for county transportation infrastructure programs, with

matching funds provided by the California
government. Smaller counties could form regional
transit agencies, pooling together funds and
resources.

Areas with fewer transportation developments and
greater automotive needs can keep their taxes low,
while areas requiring, for example, greater mass
transit spending, can increase their local tax to raise
funds and discourage unnecessary driving. Such
taxes would be set by the Board of Supervisors, which
is more responsive to the transportation needs of the
community and directly accountable to voters.

Intellectual Property and Media

The way that information is produced, disseminated,
and consumed has changed dramatically with the rise
of first television and now the internet. We feel that
allowing corporate conglomerates to exercise
monopoly-type powers over information is bad for
our culture and our democracy.

The California National Party advocates reforms to
the way licensing for radio and TV stations is carried
out to make it easier for people to start community
radio and television stations. When all media is
owned by a few corporations, minority voices are

silenced and there is no freedom of the press. Specifically:

- We support limits on the number of radio and television stations that a single entity can own.
- Equal access to internet bandwidth is extremely important, as this is now the primary avenue for consumption of news and entertainment. We strongly support net neutrality as a way to foster independent media and limit the control that gigantic, highly integrated corporations have over the information that makes its way into our homes and minds.

Similarly we must address the rules regarding how existing works can enter the public domain. While we must enable artists and makers to legally profit from their creations, over time the laws have evolved to favor perpetual corporate profits at the expense of novelty. Copyrights exist as an incentive towards innovation; extending them infinitely does nothing to spur innovation, favors monopolistic practices and creates unnecessary barriers to entry in the market. Therefore we advocate for restoring copyright laws to their original constitutional guidelines.

California shall create an arts fund in line with EU standards to fund the arts. Public art is economical and has significant economic and cultural benefits over the long term.

California will mandate that radio and television stations broadcast on publicly owned airwaves must play at least 20% music or other locally produced content by people from their local region, in order to ensure local artists have a chance at exposure and can gain traction. Media consolidation has created significant barriers to entry for artists and musicians, and has resulted in a much less competitive media market. This is bad for artists and bad for the industry itself in the long term. This proposal is based on a very successful similar law in France that has had significant positive economic and cultural impacts, while costing virtually nothing to implement.

We advocate an overhaul of patent law to encourage and reward innovation instead of erecting unnecessary barriers to entry. This includes reinstating limits on copyright, restoring the original constitutional guidelines, and eliminating copyright extensions as noted above.

Infrastructure

California's population and economy are booming, and investments in necessary infrastructure have failed to keep up. A housing crisis faces Californians in terms of availability and cost, but many other issues are interwoven with these. The influx of people and businesses requires better access to water and energy resources, along with better and more efficient transportation which allows workers to more easily commute to major employment centers while living in more affordable outlying regions. For decades, our infrastructure has been systematically starved by American politicians who see us as an economically exploitable resource, and who spend our money everywhere but here.

The California National Party believes it is time to invest in California and create the modern infrastructure needed to provide a high standard of living for our citizens, as well as to provide the foundation for continued economic expansion and business competitiveness. Our growth and development plan addresses challenges and opportunities in urban planning, transportation, clean energy production and distribution, water

conservation, communications, and disaster
prevention.

Land Use

As laid out in the Environmental plank, the California
National Party calls for the transfer of all federal
lands to California and its First Nations to be used to
meet our water, energy, and recreational needs.

At present, the federal government controls 45% of
the territory of California. Although much of this is
forests and parklands, it also includes many of our
dams, canals, and reservoirs, as well as geographic
areas necessary for renewable energy production.
This is a uniquely western problem in that the federal
government owns nearly half the land of the 11
contiguous western states, whereas east of the Rocky
Mountains only 4% of land is federally held. The
California National Party seeks to coordinate with
our neighbors to secure sovereignty over our own
respective territories.

Such lands would subsequently be administered at
the city, county, First Nation, and California level
depending on a number of factors, including historic
use, projected infrastructure needs, environmental
concerns, and existing contracts and treaties.

Water

Water usage and accessibility is a key issue for every Californian no matter their job, politics, or place of residence. Investment in water infrastructure, for example to move water from coastal desalination plants to rural farming communities, is needed to ensure access to water at reasonable prices for all communities and farms.

The California National Party therefore advocates for the following:

- Urban water collection through rainwater should be the norm, and should be incentivized in all new construction, urban and rural, where possible.
- Green roofs and other water saving technology should be mandated on all new State buildings, and added to residential building code as a requirement, with upgrade matching funds.
- Ban on neighborhood associations and other private entities fining people for not watering lawns.
- Major government-sponsored research into desalination, to make California the world leader in this technology, and so that we can

become a water exporter to dry southwest states. Desalination plants will operate as public utilities, so revenue can support state budgets in the future and repay the up-front taxpayer investment.

Energy

California's energy policies are firmly based on a recognized need to reduce greenhouse gas emissions. The California National Party supports existing initiatives to:

- Meet the 50% by 2030 renewable energy goal.
- Shift from gasoline to zero-emission vehicles that run on electricity from plug-in electric batteries and/or hydrogen fuel cells.
- Double the energy efficiency of existing buildings.
- Explore the use of renewable gas, including biomethane and biogas, as a substitute for natural gas.

In addition, we support:

- Decentralized energy generation through individual wind and solar units.

- Phased-in upgrades to California's building codes to make green building technology mandatory for new structures.
- Subsidies and incentives for property owners to upgrade existing structures, using appropriate green technology, in order to reduce the environmental impact, energy consumption, and water usage.

We will work in partnership with Californian industry through the Office of Innovation to make us a leader in green energy, and to smooth the transition to a post-carbon economy. We need focused investment into green energy and methods to reduce the carbon footprint of industry. Patents on this technology will give Californian businesses an edge in the coming post-carbon economy and be a valuable asset in their own right.

Housing and Construction

The rising cost of living poses an existential crisis for many longtime residents, favoring wealthy newcomers and real estate speculators. To ameliorate this stress we support simplification of building permits and environmental review in urban areas to support urban infill and avoid displacing residents. Environmental review should be more efficient, not less stringent, and rent control should be a mechanism to stabilize at-risk communities and limit suburban sprawl.

California can incentivize sustainable development by only providing funds for redevelopment if certain density and mixed-use requirements are met. In particular, projects featuring three or four stories of residential atop first-floor retail will be encouraged. This will facilitate car-free living on a human scale and create a large number of affordable homes. With fewer individual yards, it will be necessary to increase funding for the creation and maintenance of parks and other urban green spaces.

In addition, the California National Party advocates for the following:

- We must end racial segregation of neighborhoods in California. There should be focused investment into infrastructure, parks, schools, and public services such as street cleaning in historically marginalized communities.
- Investment in sustainable, healthy, and high-quality lower-income housing in urban blight areas.

- California must end the creation of 'poverty islands' in public housing. Low-income housing should be integrated into neighborhoods and not concentrated into low-opportunity islands.
- As the best farmlands and wildlife habitats are frequently also the most likely to be usurped by residential use, we encourage zoning policies that preserve and enhance forests, greenspace, and working farms.
- California must see to the expeditious completion of the earthquake early-alert system project, similar to Japan's, so that we can minimize deaths and injuries in the event of earthquakes.
- Encourage planting of native plant species to reduce threat of wildfire.
- Solicitation of designs and bids for a seawall at the Golden Gate of the San Francisco Bay as defense against future flooding, as called for in our Environmental plank.

Transportation

The California National Party advocates for the following:

- Investment in transportation infrastructure to end the freeway gridlock that wastes time and reduces the quality of life in many of our cities with a transportation policy that focuses on the needs of each region, based on geography and population density.
- Specifically we support a commission to investigate the feasibility of Solar Roadways.
- In urban areas, increased development and expansion of light rail in urban cores to encourage density and reduce congestion, along with intercity rail to encourage mass transit commuters from outlying suburbs.
- For increased regional urban integration, investments in freeways and automobile transit infrastructure must be part of an integrated plan, not the sole option.
- To encourage cycling, dedicated lanes separated from car traffic by a curb or other hard boundary should become the norm, to be employed in all new construction and retrofitted to existing roadways as needed. As well, other bicycle infrastructure such as secure storage should continue to develop, and cities should encourage the deployment of rental fleets where feasible.

- Regional transportation should be consolidated with the goal of increasing efficiency and removing bureaucracy, especially in areas with a number of uncoordinated transit agencies, such as the Bay Area. Such transit plans should be developed in conjunction with regional housing plans with similar simplification and streamlining of the approval process.
- Matching funding from California government for transit infrastructure more strongly tied to amount of traffic and population of surrounding area in terms of ratio to citywide population, not absolute numbers. Lower-density neighborhoods will allow local officials to either zone higher density areas around transit hubs or cover the cost of building and transit maintenance themselves.
- We support high-speed rail, and greater rail connectivity in general, across California, including the efforts by the California High-Speed Rail Authority to establish an initial working system by 2025. High-speed rail links the California nation and allows all of our people to enjoy the wide range of opportunities and experiences our great nation has to offer, with maximum efficiency and

minimal cost. Rural areas should be attached
to this by a modern bus system consolidated
around regional hubs.

Rule of Law

The California National Party supports scrapping the USA Patriot Act, which was passed in haste in the days following 9/11. It has led to the unparalleled intrusion by government agencies, often with the assistance of corporations, into the privacy of millions of Americans, most of whom have no connection to terrorism. There has been no valid rationale suggested to allow the continuation of this surveillance, which has certainly not made Californians safer from terrorist acts, most of which involve American citizens shooting at other American citizens at schools or other public places. It is time for a less intrusive and more reasoned policy for the prevention of terrorism.

- We demand greater judicial transparency and full due process for anyone accused of a crime. Indefinite detention without trial is unlawful and must not be allowed, not only for Californians, but for the many immigrants who find themselves in detention solely for immigration violations without any regard for their long-time residency, civil rights or dignity.

- Officials who have violated international human rights laws should be prosecuted and punished to the fullest extent of the law. Specifically, individuals responsible for extrajudicial rendition, the use of torture, and extrajudicial killings must be prosecuted. California must not facilitate the shielding of war criminals, including corporate, government and military officials.
- We believe that upon independence, California will join the International Criminal Court.
- We oppose racial and gender-biased enforcement of laws. We demand full equality before the law and due process for all people.

The "Global War on Terror," vigorously pursued by Republicans and approved by Democrats, has destabilized the international system, ruined any claim to credibility, and degraded national security. To repair this damage, we believe that California should:

- Advocate for all states to adopt non-interventionist foreign policies and limit military spending to 2% of GDP.
- Convene a working group on Islamophobia, to address the root causes of xenophobia and

intolerance in hopes of reducing hate crimes and wars of convenience.

- Develop an approach to mitigate the global challenges caused by millions of displaced people. This should include a humane immigration policy as well as foreign aid policies designed to stabilize fragile democracies in developing countries, as described in Prosperity and Growth.

Privacy

The Constitution of the state of California affords stronger protection of personal privacy than that of the United States, and many of our citizens feel that the War on Terror has gone too far in allowing the government to examine private lives. We oppose mass government surveillance programs and similar non-governmental actions, taken by corporations on their own behalf or in concert with the government, which impinge upon personal privacy. Therefore, we believe that California should immediately end its compliance with mass surveillance programs conducted by the CIA, DHS, DIA, FBI, NSA, any other Federal agency, or their foreign and corporate allies.

As technology becomes more pervasive and more personal information becomes available on the web, it is becoming increasingly difficult for citizens to monitor their online footprint and maintain their privacy. This can have significant negative impacts, particularly on young people. Therefore, the California National Party supports an individual's right to have one's personal information as well as any other content, such as electronic messages or photographs, deleted and removed from any publically-accessible website, server, or database upon request.

- We oppose all government demands for manufacturers of software and electronic devices to include encryption "back doors". Back doors undermine security, contribute to the rise of a surveillance state, and violate the right to privacy of consumers.
- We support the "right to be forgotten," as pioneered by the European Union. All citizens should have the ability to have Google and all other websites remove information about them upon request.
- California must provide protection for whistleblowers and others who expose

corruption, including strong "Shield Laws" for journalists and other whistleblowers.

- We advocate stronger restrictions on the power of credit reporting agencies, and the situations in which a credit report can be obtained. Specifically, potential employers should not be able to demand a credit report unless it has a direct bearing on job performance or if there is a security risk.

- We support regulation of personal, commercial and governmental drones as necessary to preserve personal privacy.

Gun Rights and Regulation

Gun policy should be based on the recognition that different areas of California have varying issues and social attitudes related to firearms. The vast majority of gun related crimes take place in two dozen California counties, while many have had zero or one murder over the course of several years. Crime prevention strategies must be based on the realities of each specific community being served and weighed against the need for people to defend themselves and their families. Gun policy in California cannot be successful with a one-size-fits-all approach.

Therefore, the California National Party supports the following policies:

- California-wide gun laws should be reduced in number and scope and greater regulatory power given to individual counties. Those with more restrictive policies must respect the rights of other counties to have more permissive laws, and vice versa. City laws may be more but not less restrictive than county laws.
- California will establish a registration system for sellers, buyers, and owners, similar to regulations necessary for automobile use and ownership. Like a driver's license, those applying for a firearms permit would be required to pass a written exam and demonstration of skill and responsibility. This would be administered at the county level through the sheriff's department.
- Sellers can sell to buyers who reside or are employed in that county, or to California residents of other counties, provided they are not sold anything that is banned in the buyer's home county or city.
- The required waiting period under California law will be reduced from the current 10 days

to five days, while individual counties may choose to extend this period to no more than two weeks.

- We support a California-wide ban on fully automatic weapons. Semi-automatic weapons, ammunition restrictions, magazine capacity restrictions, and handgun laws would be defined by each county, as would bullet microstamping requirements.
- California law will require that special permits must be issued for assault rifles. Each county sheriff's office will issue such permits and regulate local sales. An individual with that permit must possess a current military, law enforcement, or firearm instructor certification. Individuals wishing to own an assault rifle must pass a psychological evaluation and not have any felonies on their record.
- After the assault rifle permit is in place, the California National Party supports eliminating the featureless grip and the welded magazine regulations.
- Violations of these intercounty regulations, such as selling firearms or ammunition in counties in which they are illegal or to buyers who reside in such counties, as well as transferring firearms without reporting a

change in registered ownership, will be met
with severe legal penalties.

We also defend many currently existing California
gun laws, such as:

- The "may issue" policy on concealed carry
  permits through each county's sheriff, as well
  as laws protecting open carry in
  unincorporated rural areas where not
  prohibited by local ordinance.
- Castle doctrine for purposes of self-defense
  within one's home.
- Red flag laws establishing Extreme Risk
  Protection Orders by which police or family
  members can petition a court to confiscate
  weapons for a certain period of time from
  those deemed a threat to themselves or others.
- While California remains part of the United
  States, our laws must adhere to the
  interpretations of Second Amendment handed
  down from the Supreme Court of the United
  States.

California also has a problem with the trafficking of
illegal guns from other states. The California National
Party supports better enforcement of our current

laws, and California should post signs at the borders to inform people of our gun laws and the penalties for trafficking weapons. We should allow people from other states to surrender those guns at the Inspection Point to be stored at an armory free of charge, or to be mailed back to the owner's home state at their expense.

Policing Reform

While most police are dedicated civil servants, enough are corrupt and abusing their power without sufficient oversight that there is a need for communities to be able to maintain oversight of those authorized by the government to use lethal force. The California National Party believes that California should:

- Provide state-level guidance and legal authority for community oversight of police in both Charter and General Law cities.
- Establish state-level penalties for individual officers who abuse their power.
- Create a statewide database of officers banned from working in any public safety jobs.
- Establish state-level penalties for city departments and county sheriffs that fail to

follow through with sanctions on individuals and that hire a banned individual.

- For new recruits, require a minimum of an Associate's degree, preferably in Criminal Justice, that include at least 4 classes on racial issues.
- For current police officers, implement new ongoing training that addresses implicit bias and historical causes of inequality.
- Expand and modernize emergency medical response systems, including exploring the idea of partnering police with mental health professionals on medical or mental health emergency calls.
- Increase funding of emergency medical and fire response systems, including salaries and fringe benefits that will make those public safety positions competitive with police.

Bail Reform

The California National Party opposes a pre-trial system that disproportionately incarcerates and punishes the poor. The money bail system allows the rich to avoid the inconvenience of pre-trial detention while ruining the lives of those who cannot afford to pay. Our long-term goal is to end indefinite and bail-

contingent pre-trial detention and abolish the for-
profit bail industry.

We support California's efforts to addresses racial
and economic disparities in the justice system and
endorse Senate Bill SB-10 Bail: Pretrial Release. In
addition, California must ban confiscation of assets
by law enforcement without due process. This creates
perverse incentives for law enforcement and, like
many elements of the War on Drugs, is most
commonly targeted against non-whites.

Correctional Reform

People of color -- especially African Americans,
Latinos, and First Nations -- are disproportionately
arrested, tried, and convicted for crimes, resulting in
even non-violent and low-level offenses destroying
far too many lives, and violating the principle that the
punishment should fit the crime.

The California National Party believes that California
should:

- Allow people convicted of crimes to vote, and
  reinstate that right to the many from whom it
  has been stripped.

- "Ban the Box" and prevent both public and private employers from requiring job applicants to state whether they have been convicted of a felony or a misdemeanor.
- Decriminalize use of all recreational drugs and establish adequately-funded substance abuse treatment programs and rehabilitation clinics in every county.
- Provide amnesty and criminal record expungement of all convictions for drinking in public, drug possession, and low-level possession for sale.
- Expunge all juvenile criminal records of all individuals who, following their release, reach the age of 21 or have 5 consecutive years without any criminal indictments.
- Disincentivize overcharging by District Attorneys and issue a state mandate to focus prosecutions on violent and white collar crimes.
- Expand Public Defender offices and make their salaries and staff levels equivalent to those of prosecutors.
- Establish a dedicated statewide re-entry and anti-recidivism body separate from CDCR that incorporates both job training and trauma-informed therapy into its services.

- Decrease funding of the California Department
  of Corrections and Rehabilitation, while
  increasing funding of probation and parole
  systems.
- Mandate all probation and parole contracts for
  anti-recidivism, substance abuse treatment,
  and mental or physical healthcare services go
  to the Departments of Education, Public
  Health, or Health and Human Services.

Judicial Funding and Access

Equality under the law requires not only good laws,
but access to the judicial system. Despite this, the
court system of California is chronically underfunded
and ignored. This delays trials and results in both
urban overcrowding and the need for rural residents
to travel additional miles and spend many hours to
gain access to the justice system. Improvements for
ADA compliance have been neglected, and
construction, especial in rural counties, of new court
structures has been long delayed. In addition to
infrastructure needs, the basic duties of the court
system, such as adjudicating cases both criminal and
civil, have become monumentally backlogged. This
has been exacerbated by layoffs and stagnant, or even
unpaid, wages to court officers and workers such as
interpreters, court clerks, and judges.

Such fiscal uncertainty in one of the largest judicial systems in the world is unacceptable. Therefore, the California National Party proposes a minimum funding mandate for the judiciary of no less than 1.5% of any California budget. (In the last decade, funding has hovered around 1.3%-1.4%.) In times of economic strength, the budget may set aside funds beyond this 1.5% minimum to be stored in an exclusive judicial fund to be tapped for unforeseen projects, new infrastructure, or to make up for shortfalls in later budgets during times of economic decline; however, this fund must be used only for the judiciary, and not raided for other government expenditures.

Legislative and Electoral Reform

Ending Corporate Personhood

A legal challenge as to whether the State of California had the power to tax a railroad fencing resulted in the finding, written as a headnote by a court clerk in 1866, that corporations are entitled to equal protection under the law, and can be accorded the same rights as persons.

Over time, legal statutes and high court decisions have granted increasing rights to corporations resulting in the notion of corporate personhood, which is the idea that corporations should enjoy the legal status and protections created for people. Its effect is that corporations and business interests can use their massive resources to compete with voting individuals for the control of public policy. This is problematic because the intent of a governmental enterprise is the well being of the constituents that it serves, while the intent of a corporate enterprise is to earn the highest possible revenue with lowest possible expenditure to produce the highest possible profits for their owners and investors The interests of

the public as persons thus become vulnerable to the
rights of corporations to spend money at incredibly
high levels to affect political matters which can
advance their interests. The inevitable result is that
public gains become privatized; while public losses
are socialized, with little regard for the best interests
of society.

In the later case of *Buckley vs. Valeo*, 1976, the United
States ruled that limits on campaign spending
violated the First Amendment rights of free speech by
prohibiting the quantity of expression. It was judged
that corporations had as much right as citizens to
spend as they choose to promote a political message,
lest their right to free speech be abridged. Again, the
interests of the wealthy and/or well organized (this
includes organized labor-unions) have prevented an
equal ability for individuals to speak to one another
or to an elected representative.

In 2010, the United States Supreme Court extended
this logic in *Citizens United v. FEC*, which prohibited
any limitation on spending by all entities in political
campaigns as a violation of their rights to free speech
under the First Amendment. In essence, corporations
and other organizations, who are capable of spending
significantly higher sums on political campaigns, can

outspend citizens and the public with their vast resources in order to influence elections.

It is therefore the position of the California National Party to support challenges to the legal notion of corporate personhood, as well as to endorse laws and practices within California that recognize the political rights of human beings over artificial corporate entities.

Campaign Finance Reform

Perhaps the longest standing flaw in the United States political system is how parties and campaigns are privately financed, resulting in a concentration of political power with the wealthy. This was exacerbated by the Supreme Court's decisions in Citizens United and Buckley v. Valeo which paved the way for the Super PACs of today.

The California National Party endorses strictly limiting private financing of candidates, political parties and other political entities, including a reversal of Citizens United, to reduce the influence of entities other than individual constituents. There are many structures used in Europe and Israel where governments pay for the operation of parties and campaigns for elected offices. We believe we need to use these as a guide for establishing a more equitable campaign process.

Open Source Voting

The California National Party believes it is essential that the hardware and software we use for gathering, aggregating, and reporting votes to elect public officials need to be secure, accessible, auditable, and transparent.

For this reason we advocate for the adoption of open source voting platforms such as the one being defined by San Francisco's Open Source Voting System Project. Such a system would include:

- A touch-screen voter station where the voter selects their choices.
- Alternative voter stations that include accessible features such as sip and puff input, a keyboard for write-in votes, voice activation, synchronized audio and video, joystick input, tactile buttons, etc.
- A human- and machine-readable printed ballot that the voter would review for accuracy.
- A scanner to capture the ballot's image as well as to record the voter's selections.

The actual equipment to collect and tabulate results should primarily include OSI-approved copyleft open source software. Because the source code is publically viewable, claims about its integrity and security are independently-verifiable as compared to "secret" proprietary software.

Ranked Choice Voting

Following the lead of cities like Berkeley, Oakland, and San Francisco, the California National Party encourages the statewide adoption of Ranked Choice Voting.

With Ranked Choice Voting, also called Instant Runoff Voting, voters rank candidates in order of choice: 1st choice, 2nd choice, and so on. At tabulation time, if no candidate receives a majority of 1st-choice votes, the candidate with the least number of 1st-choice votes is eliminated and their votes recast for the voters' 2nd-choice picks. This elimination and retabulation process continues until there are two candidates left in the race; the one with the most votes is declared the winner.

We believe that this system has many advantages:
- Encourages candidates to build a coalition of support and avoid negative campaigning

because they may need voters to consider
them as their 2nd or 3rd choices.

- Results in a winning candidate supported by
  the majority of voters.
- Provides more choices to voters while
  minimizing strategic voting.
- Saves money when it replaces primaries or
  runoffs.

Local Government Reform

The complexity and diversity of California requires
that we recognize and respect that different regions
face many specific, localized needs and obstacles. For
many rural and unincorporated communities—even
in counties with a great deal of urban development—
the Board of Supervisors and other county officials
are the most direct government for citizens. The
California National Party will support candidates at
the local, county, and California level that will fight to
bring more accountability to local officials.

We will work to convert all counties with populations
greater than 200,000 into charter counties instead of
general law, either by voter initiative or through the
board itself, so they may set their own number of
supervisors. Expanding the number of Supervisors in
large counties will allow rural and unincorporated

voters a greater voice in county representation which
tends to affect their lives more directly than those
who live in incorporated cities and towns. We
propose the following minimum number of
supervisors based on population, although counties
may expand this number to meet their needs:

- 5 supervisors for counties with a
  population below 200,000
- 7 supervisors for counties between
  200,000 and 700,000 people
- 9 supervisors for between 700,000 and
  1.5 million
- 11 supervisors for 1.5 to 5 million
- 13 supervisors for 5 to 10 million
- 15 supervisors for over 10 million
  people

Such charter counties would also be free to locally
experiment with different models of county
governance—for example, a separate county
executive office—provided they are in compliance
with California electoral law and are not
disenfranchising groups of voters or designed to give
undue power to certain parties, organizations, or
industries. The Secretary of State will oversee
counties in terms of electoral compliance, but we

support existing law that such structural government variations would be the choice of local voters and not require external approval. We support the right of counties, especially less populated rural ones, to construct regional plans for issues such as transportation, or to merge together into larger counties if they so desire.

Proportional Representation in the Senate

The California National Party proposes that California retain legislative bicameralism, but convert the Senate into a system of Party List Proportional Representation. This is by far the most common form of proportional representation in the world, numerous variants of which are used, especially in Europe. This would require an amendment to the California Constitution, either by the initiative process or through the support of two-thirds of the present legislature. The Assembly would remain based on district representation for the unique needs of that area, while the Senate would represent the ideological variation of California's entire population.

Election for Senate would be by all California voters, not by district. Each party would run a slate of up to

40 candidates in a specific order. How each party determines this-- by party primary, either closed or open to unaffiliated voters, local districts elections, etc.-- is up to the party and its members. Each party receives one Senate seat per 2.5% (1/40th of 40 Senators) of the total vote, with remainder determined by Largest Remainder Method. This allows smaller parties that have a following throughout California, but not concentrated in any one place, representation in legislating proportional to its following, while locally large parties and independent candidates also can still gain senate seats.

We believe that there are numerous strategic benefits to this approach to reform:

- First, simplicity and minimal change. California voters would chafe at losing an elected executive branch or a direct district representative. But there is no reason to have two bodies in the legislature elected by the same method, the Senate simply having more populous, and thus more unmanageable and unrepresentative, districts. This change gives a reason again for a bicameral legislative branch post-Reynolds v. Sims, which ended Senators as county representatives.

- Second, alliances with other groups. It is is highly probable that all alternative parties of California, likely along with the Republican Party, would benefit in terms of representation from such a system and can hopefully be expected to support this reform, along with many unaffiliated voters—in essence, anyone without a vested interest in the Democratic Party's monopoly of power throughout the executive and legislative branch. Indeed, many of those in the Democratic Party who feel disenfranchised by the party establishment may also see reason to support it. Since it seems unlikely that the Democratic-controlled legislature will voluntarily undertake such an action with the necessary supermajority, this reform will likely require a direct initiative and broad support.

Increase Size of Legislature

At present, each member of the 80 person Assembly must represent roughly half a million human beings, while those of the 40 person Senate therefore represent nearly a million. Many members are forced to represent multiple counties across diverse regions, with boundaries drawn not based on the shared interests of the population, but with the interests of the two-party system in mind. This is in fact representation in name only.

The California National Party believes that expanding the size of the Assembly would enable each member to represent, and be more directly accountable to, a smaller group of Californians with shared economic, social, and geographic conditions. Rather than enshrine a set number of Assembly members, they can be required by law to represent an average of no more than 100,000 constituents. As the population increases, members are added to the Assembly once the average number surpasses 100,000. As is done now, district lines will be redrawn after each decennial census by an independent commission selected specifically and solely for that purpose, although ideally the California Citizens Redistricting Commission, which presently is designed to reinforce an assumed two party system, would be reformed. Variants of this dynamic increase to the legislature as needed are performed by a number of nations, e.g. Germany and the Scandinavian countries.

At present, such a California Assembly would be comprised of 397 members. This would place us roughly on par with many similar democracies. Rural areas would be better represented as districts would not be forced to encompass such diverse interests, while densely populated urban areas benefit from increased representative access.

Likewise, increasing the size of the California Senate to 50 Senators will enable proportional representation in a manner that is intuitive—2% of total vote equals one Senator—as well as expanding the range of voices which may be heard.

Independence

There comes a time in the history of many nations when a distinct people must pursue the path of self-reliance for their own survival. A course which may have once been unwise and unthinkable can become necessary and inevitable. California has reached such a point in its history. A land of extensive geographic, human, and financial diversity, replete with natural resources, home to a population of nearly 40 million people, and an over $2.75 trillion economy, cannot reasonably be called anything but a nation. An inevitable consequence of this is that California has problems of a national scale that can only be successfully solved with the power and authority of an independent republic.

Increasingly, Californians are unable to rely on the federal government to effectively secure their well-being, while our revenue and income is used to fund projects throughout the United States and push for its interests (military, economic, geopolitical) around the globe. This is exacerbated by a partisan political and electoral structure that can afford to openly disregard our needs, since in both the Senate and electing the President, our voice is effectively silenced.

Californians must recognize that no one will look out for our interests unless we do so ourselves.

To this end, the California National Party supports constructing an enduring program of strengthening California while simultaneously laying the groundwork for ever greater autonomy, self-determination, and ultimately independence with recognition by the United Nations, the United States, and other actors in the international community. This will require the assent and cooperation of the government and people of the United States, and therefore California must prepare to enter good faith negotiations with the federal government to assure a mutually agreed upon course for the peaceful legal and political separation of our respective countries.

While many Americans may question our motivations, we ask that they look back on and respect their own past to see a national moment when "it becomes necessary for one People to dissolve the Political Bands which have connected them with another, and to assume among the Powers of the Earth, the separate and equal Station to which the Laws of Nature and of Nature's God entitle them." At such times, it is the right of that people to "institute new Government, laying its Foundation on such Principles, and organizing its Powers in such Form, as to them shall seem most likely to effect their Safety and Happiness." We in California see the wisdom of these words today and sincerely hope that the people of the United States will also continue to cherish their own founding principles.

The California National Party lays out three legal, potentially complementary, paths to ultimate independence. Each requires petition by the people of California, by referendum and/or through our elected representatives, and consent by the United States Congress and President, although at no stage is a constitutional amendment required:

- Admission of California into the United States was a legislative act that can be undone in the same fashion; states are only constitutionally forbidden to leave the United States unilaterally, but can with "consent of the states," see Supreme Court decision Texas vs. White.
- Seek a change of status within the federal system away from full statehood toward modified commonwealth status, while developing phased and progressive steps of

growing autonomy toward independence as was done with the United States' former colonial possessions of Cuba, the Philippines, etc.

- Negotiate through the United Nations to be recognized as part of the Compact of Free Association with the United States, an international agreement by which the United States government is obligated "to promote the development of the people of the Trust Territory toward self-government or independence as appropriate to the particular circumstances of the Trust Territory and its peoples and the freely expressed wishes of the peoples concerned."

We therefore advocate a popular referendum on independence once the people of California have had adequate time and reflection to embrace the benefits of independence. Should the people of California choose to support independence for the California Republic, we call upon the elected representatives of California to move with all deliberate speed to implement that decision and work with our neighbors to assure a peaceful and smooth transition.

On Citizenship

All persons born in California shall become California nationals, eligible for California citizenship should they desire it. No person shall ever be forced to accept the Californian citizenship to which they are entitled, nor should any person lose their United States citizenship or immigration status as a result of independence. California nationals serving in the Armed Forces of the United States will also immediately be eligible for California citizenship.

California Permanent Residents who have maintained residency in California for no less than 5 years shall also be deemed as eligible for California citizenship. California residents who have lived here continuously for 1 year at the time of independence will be eligible for permanent residency and become eligible for citizenship after 5 years.

Constitutional Convention

We call for a new national constitutional convention to be held within six months of a successful vote for independence by the people of California. A delegation shall be sent from each county as well as Californian First Nations to this convention with the goal of creating the legal framework and delineation of powers to form a new national government. This document will become the supreme law of the land if and when it is approved by 60% of the citizens of California.

Our new national government will thereby become limited to certain denoted powers which shall be determined at the constitutional convention and which shall be considerably circumscribed compared to the coercive federalism which has defined United States government policy since at least the middle of the 20th century.

On The Military

We believe that the Republic of California's military needs can best be served through a highly organized national militia with a core professional army, based on the Swiss model, wherein the people of California are the military. This model will save us many billions of dollars per year, build a sense of national pride and identity, and ensure our defense.

All citizens will be expected to register for military service upon turning 18. This militia will be run similarly to the current national guard, in which citizen-soldiers undergo basic training and then will be required to attend specific short training exercises on a periodic basis. Persons who object to military service on religious or moral grounds may serve in a civilian peace corps instead. Citizens with physical disabilities preventing service in the field will have the option to serve in other capacities or in the peace corps. After the age of 20 all citizens will be expected to report for 2 weeks out of every year for training and service. This service will be paid. Hardship will allow deferment but the time must be made up as soon as the hardship has ended.

California will maintain a small professional military, made up of the best of the best, who want to make a career out of military service. This cadre of experienced professional soldiers will form the core of our national military should we need to mobilize on a large scale to defend ourselves. The professional military forces will include naval, air, and ground forces.

The California National Party supports maintaining friendly relations with the United States based on the principles of cooperation and supporting the goals of economic growth and the common defense. California will enter mutual defense treaties with other nations but will not participate in military interventions.

Accordingly, the California National Party supports entering into military base agreements, which are known as Status of Force Agreements, with the United States whereby American military installations located in California may be leased to the United States, unrestricted and at no-cost, for 25 years with final terms to be negotiated. After the 25 year period has elapsed, a reasonable use fee for the land and airspace under lease will be introduced.